"What a moving and unusual book *The Comedown* is! A long poem, or perhaps a memoir in verse, or a dramatic monologue, it is both playful and yet revealing, honest and philosophical, formally innovative and yet direct. Marks shows us human life from childhood to parenthood, from loneliness to marriage:

> We struggle
> We love each other

"At the center of this work, the unforgettable image of a young child watching his father accidentally light himself on fire. From there, the contradictions come:

> The reason to stay
> is the desire to leave.

"And from contradiction comes wisdom:

> reality is the best
> metaphor for reality.

"Comes poetry:

> Text becoming body

"Comes transformation. How? Because Justin Marks is willing to be vulnerable, he is able to question what poetry can do—what language itself can do—to depict the drama of the human mind:

> a disordered mind
> is its own
> order

"Indeed. Herein contradiction challenges the form, makes the poet search for new forms, makes out of fragments a transformation."
—**Ilya Kaminsky, author of *Dancing in Odessa***

"Part confession, part tirade, part commentary, Justin Marks' third poetry collection *The Comedown*, is a riveting, taut exploration into the toxic matrix of masculinity, capitalism, illness, the doldrums of perceived mediocrity, and the travails of the restless, seeking mind. Like a diamond drill bit, Marks bores into the heart of the matter: dissolution of the self, of marriage, of fatherhood, of youth, of the ego with precision, humor, and unflinching candor to expose stark beauty in a life lived hard despite its accumulated traumas and vices. His singular voice contends with the universality of existential dread without artifice or grandeur, but rather in the most intimate, nearly imperceptible moments that render us human—fallible, but full of grace."
—**Su Hwang, author of *Bodega***

# THE COMEDOWN

Copyright © Justin Marks 2020
All rights reserved

First published by Publishing Genius Press
Atlanta, Georgia
publishinggenius.com
@pubgen

ISBN 978-1-945028-33-5

All photos by the author
on Instagram @thecomedown2020
Book design by Adam Robinson

# THE COMEDOWN

## Justin Marks

Publishing Genius Press
Atlanta ▪ Georgia ▪ USA

CONTENTS

The Comedown // 1

*for Meri*

As a person I'm a fiction     A heart

of vomit     Huge amounts

of protein

Scared     Sacred

The difference is simple

transposition

Getting high in bathrooms

Applying for jobs

Everything I do

I do for approval

Continuous movement

A need beyond my ability

I go to an anonymous government building to submit my documents. There are no clocks. They make you turn off your phone. I stand in line for what feels like a very long time. I read a few pages of a book by Anne Boyer.

"We're good—cheering content providers, boring despots," she says.

"History dwindles," she says.

The line starts moving. It splits into two lines.

The people on the right are given blue cards with numbers. People on the left, red with numbers.

I have a red card.

I don't know what any of this means.

I write this all inside the back cover of Boyer's book until my number comes up.

In meetings at work I write stuff in my notebook like:

> *Be smart*
> *about being*
> *smart*

Tamped wrists                               Technicolor pasts

What I think is a man beating a child
is really a blonde dog's tail wagging
in the backseat of a dark car

The people I'm closest to—I don't know
how to take them seriously

A tragedy

A terrible thing that happens
then is just a thing

that happened

I'm the way
I've learned to be

An unfortunate
accident

I wallow in myself
to forget myself

This morning a cap fell off my tooth
that is the majority of my tooth

I keep it
in a sandwich bag

If your link says NSFW
I will click on it
at work

What I'm trying to avoid saying is all the terrible
things I imagine others think about me

Everything my fucked up
perception tells me

Emotions I can't
access—

joy
missed

When someone asks me a question
my immediate response is *no*

    A delusion of grandeur
    that's mediocre

        A nucleus burning
        inside itself

    Help that doesn't help

To prevent prostate cancer
jerk off at least 3 times a week

        A medical excuse
        to mask

        the loneliness

        A future that's always
        about to end

        #TGIF

A disordered mind
is its own
order

A slip from one body
to a text

What I feel is
unreliable

Nothing is good
unless it's undeniably great
is an idea I'm trying to escape

Pleasure varied
but never increased

Emotion
exhausts me

Reality is the best
metaphor for reality

More insidious
than ecstatic

More energy
than talent

Birth
        Sex
                Death

The high
I'm chasing

Things go my way
I want them more my way

A cloud of comets enclosing
a solar system

A world that syncs up, but not quite,
is broken but works anyway

Reading that begets writing that begets reading
that begets writing that begets what you're holding

A universe
experiencing itself

A spotty connection

I select a language I don't speak
as the language of the ATM

More fun for my lack
of understanding

Silence
A poet is speaking

10,000 species
are going extinct

A bug
in the system

The reason to stay
is the desire to leave

This is my listening face
It's terrible
Like all my faces

❖

In the crowd, a path will appear
It will appear
or you will make it

❖

I wish you could see the rain
on my screen as I text you

How purposeful it is
to my diction

❖

I'm scared and overly self
-protective working on a form
of extreme moderation

Its practice

❖

I'm married
but still fantasize
about meeting *the one*

There are so many ones

❖

That my (in)actions affect others is still not something I fully grasp

❖

Little white light that's gonna show my religion

Strange distance

Hit me with your money

❖

*Text, and art, like a human being, bends the artificial borders of identity*

❖

My barber's name is Frank

The world I grew up in was vast beyond my comprehension. And small.

The farmer's fields. A lone tractor. A crop-duster buzzing our house to unleash a yellow mist of pesticide on the field across the street.

When I was little I'd run outside and wave up at the plane and the pilot would rock his wings from side-to-side back at me.

We had chickens and a huge garden that gave us vegetables.

The chickens gave us eggs. In the summer we slaughtered them. My father tied them upside down by their feet on a pole in the yard and chopped off their heads with an axe. They flapped madly until he untied them and then they'd walk around, headless, still somehow pecking. But all that banging against the pole, we later discovered, bruised the meat.

The next year Dad tried something different. He walked into the coop, grabbed a chicken by its feet and neck, pulled and twisted. He handed it to my mother who would dip it in a pot of boiling water to loosen the pores and she'd pull the feathers.

Clean, simple, primal. Terrifying. Sublime.

As the day went on, the chickens must have sensed my father's adrenaline, smelled the death. They grew agitated, my father became more aggressive. Eventually he emerged from the coop with a head in one hand, body in the other.

A remarkable lack of blood.

    People want things to end
    but not really
    Not, like, forever

    *Go down on history*, I say
    I mean, *in*

    Go
    different ways

    *The options are limitless*
    says my horoscope

There are these memories I've been trying to figure out what to do with. Like when I was a kid out looking for things to shoot with my bb gun and saw a baby bird in a nest in the rafter of our barn with its neck stretched out, mouth open, waiting for its mother to return with food. I shot it. Its little cheeps slowed then stopped, as if merely its batteries had run down, and I turned back to the house, nauseous with shame, to pretend it never happened.

    The only way I know to write
    is to read

    What I like about that is
    the different words I get to use

    That I get to change

    The murkiness
    of who or what it is

    I'm praying to

Illness. Lots of illness. Nothing chronic or life threatening. But persistent. Miserable. Like waking up with the worst hangover every day. Except I was just a kid.

I wasn't alone in my loneliness. I had friends. Damaged ones. We didn't treat each other very well.

We smoked weed. And other things. Formed habits. We convinced each other to date girls we didn't want to date then ridiculed each other for dating them. Humiliation. Shame. Presumed short-term safety in identifying each other as more vulnerable. The psychology of the traumatized lacking sympathy for each other.

>   It's what bound us.
>   Was all we knew.
>
>   The limits of the language we had
>   to work with.

Rage. Violence felt like the only way. Against myself. From age seven onward. On display to anyone who would pay attention—teachers, my parents, people who should have known how to help but couldn't say much other than, "What's wrong with you? Why are you like this? Why can't you control yourself?" The favorite toys I threw and smashed to pieces. Holes punched into walls, the cheap survival knife I stabbed into them over and over trying to kill I don't know what—my fear, my helplessness, myself, my shame. Or maybe it was exhaustion I was seeking, depletion, because at a certain point whatever I was angry about no longer mattered, was forgotten. And I would sleep the most revitalizing sleep.

"Maybe we all got one big soul who everybody's a part of," says a character in one of my favorite movies. "One big self. Everyone looking for salvation by themselves."

    Empathy     Isolation

    that can't be overcome

    That feels right

    I want that desperately
    not to feel right

    I want
    to feel closeness
    and have it last

    Have it come from
    something other than exhaustion, endless

    depths of aimless anger

    The dead thud
    of solid objects coming into contact
    at high velocity

I never know what I'm supposed to be doing, or why. Another drink. More food. Wanting things just to want them. The other night I got very drunk while my wife and I were over at a friend's house and all our kids were playing together. I would like to tell you what happened next, but can't remember. All I know is I woke up in my bed the next morning, miraculously not too hungover, and started getting the kids ready for school. My wife looked at me, exhausted, and told me how she'd been up half the night because the kids refused to stay in their beds. "And you," she said, "you were a different story. We'll talk about you later."

Whatever you say I am
is what I am

A child holding a lighter
A really cool weather event

I'll be that

The trauma and the story
of the trauma I was told

*Your touch*
*is intimidating*

*It feels too good*

is what I think when my wife touches me

Massive gaps
in my development

Unidentified signals
from deep space

Under the skin
is more skin

Increasingly sensitive

Nary a wound salt
water can't heal

You people who set rules
for yourselves and follow them—
how do you do that?

I express gratitude
Expect love and praise

Get pissed when
I don't get it

See people being happy and act
incredulous

Little explosions that keep the engine going

Pain that lingers long
after the wound is inflicted—

You amaze me

I'd like to be more sober

Less afraid

Have clear

memories of each evening

I'd like you to think

I'm brilliant

A genius

Someone who

exercises regularly

I never know what to believe. One of my first memories is being taken for a ride on my father's motorcycle, a Triumph. I was two, maybe three. We rode around our large rural yard. It was raining. There was no front fender so the rain and mud sprayed up on our faces. My father sat me in front of him and held me with his legs. He had mounted a bracket on the gas tank for me to hold on to. When we came back in the house he helped me take off my wet shoes and my mother removed my dirty clothes. Neither of them remembers any of this. Each of us our own unreliable narrator.

"Memoirs are just memories," my uncle once told me. "What do we do with the things we forget?"

He's a combat veteran. Has seen more people killed than he can remember. He has killed. He knows these things. But that doesn't change the lives and deaths he knows he has forgotten.

"Keep looking for reality," says Jany in Kathy Acker's *Blood and Guts in High School*. "You'll drive yourself crazier and crazier."

"Shame on you," says my career coach, "if every single moment you're not thinking, 'What next?'"

Or maybe my first memory is sitting at the foot of the stairs, not more than 2 years old, crying hysterically, immense amounts of snot coming from my nose. My mother, exasperated, disgusted, saying to my father, "Would you just do something about him?"

If nature has taught me anything
it's ambivalence

Nature is neither
cruel nor
loving

It is

is

The city feels empty
I go to work
Do as little as possible
Go home


Right on?

Write on

When I get home at night
I remove my bag

A huge weight
lifted

In the morning I
put it back on

Deeply self-conscious
Insecure

Nervous not
because I'm afraid
(though that too)

but because I don't
know how
to behave

What
to do

Money is an energy
An existential tagline

Money is current

You could make a pun on currency
but not quite

Money is an energy
nonetheless

Dark space     Dark water

A long silent drive

Dark matter(s)

The methods of one wor(l)d revealing
the hidden harmonies of another

A lotto ticket that occupies
        my pocket

My payment has not arrived

What I want to be is
out of the way

Copulate with
abandon because

abandon is all

that will have me

What I want to feel is
ecstatic

all the time

Special

Use big words and never
second guess myself

Look in the mirror
as little as possible

Somewhere in the scribble
of my signature
is my name

❖

My stiff
body

My sour
stomach

❖

I hold my body wrong
and live
in pain

My pain
amuses me

❖

There's my intention
and then
there's what happens

❖

First thought
worst thought

is the first thought I have
every morning

Trust issues
galore

❖

Fear has been a great
motivator for me

I'm told

So ready
to be wronged

Ill prepared
for any weather

❖

When I'm alone
I'm most

relaxed

Escape from self
that asserts the self

all the more strongly

Water that takes
its route

To sit and talk
makes me extremely nervous

Good behavior is thinking
of all the horrible things

I could do

then not
doing them

❖

Ambition
is stupid

Nothing's as bad
as I thought it would be

❖

The house is quiet
I'm alone

I'm at the office now, feeling hungover, staring at a computer screen. I haven't had a drink in a week but that doesn't seem to matter. I'm certain I'm about to get fired. I'm certain I'll never escape this anxiety, this feeling that any moment now I'll face a terrible reckoning.

My hearing is attuned to the slightest sound of openings. Ready to begin. Which is what I like doing best. Beginning. Before the desperate fear of work sets in. The pretense of honesty. Cloud millions.

Self-diagnosis: Patient (that's ME) suffers from continuous disruption of circadian rhythms. Wacked out fantasies. All the different ways to go with this. Steps to unwind. Average existence in which my self-loathing knows no end. Struggle for connection. The kind of thing that keeps going. Like Lil Wayne and the 12 page, 35 minute rap that was the end of everything he'd written. Now it's all freestyle. A beat and whatever comes to mind. A middle aged white dude (ME) talking about 21st century hip-hop. An individual moving at a constant velocity matching its direction to that of its neighbors within a certain radius. List all your character defects, the promise goes, and you'll find freedom, peace and happiness. Love and be loved well.

What a mess. We're such a fucking mess. Candy that tastes like weekdays. When things get emotional, the fluids flow. The blood and the grief. A flip from the throng to an organized swarm. I look nothing like I feel in pictures. But please, don't make me get naked. You wouldn't like me when I'm naked.

Tonight my body feels impossibly tight. Like I'll never sleep. Like I need a drink.

I get up, twist my wedding ring around my finger, drop it. Pick it up and slide it back on. Stare at the dent it made in the carpet. Take a long, very hot shower. Stretch. Touch my toes. Let the water loosen my muscles until I feel a wave of sleep form.

I get out. Weigh myself. Don't like the number on the scale. Sneak back into bed, quiet, careful not to wake my wife, the light of my phone guiding me. Drift off.

In this, my 40th year
driving long distances should be
considered exercise

Looking at you, your faces, your eyes
closed is my relief

which is creepy

Me staring at strangers
the strangers not knowing

or maybe they do

I don't deserve
such relief

I'm jealous
of other people's
addictions

Their recovery

I look at my wife and think
*I want you*
but I'm scared

*I want you I want you I want you*

and so lie here un
-approachable, my face
in a book

Uptight in the moment
Regretful after

A step across
a dark threshold

The only way I know to write

is to read

An attempt to

connect to

something

bigger than myself

this I

that I

mainly fuck up

Everything is inevitable. I write that and realize I write too much in absolutes.

*You wind up becoming who you are.* David Foster Wallace said something along those lines.

At first I typed, *You wind up becoming who you ate.*

I'm an Aries, I say to no one in particular, the first sign of the zodiac, the original fire. I use tones that are not honest. I'm often polite when all I want to do is scream. Several people have received texts from me that say, *My arrival is imminent.*

But it takes time. This person you're waiting to become is in no rush. I'm in no rush.

My father accidentally
lighting himself on fire

in front of me when I was four

Strange encounters
with inappropriate
adults

Their illegal
activities

I learned from an early age
to be silent

Keep secrets

Be the lesser character

Knew that if I said the wrong thing
to the right people

the right thing
to the wrong people

the wrong thing
to the wrong people

I could ruin lives

After a while
even strangers
look familiar

My father standing
at the kitchen counter

shirtless, freshly showered,
hair slicked back

like a minor god—
imperfect—

de-seeding his weed

rolling joints
for whatever

trip we were about to take

Fun is embarrassing

Booze and anger
my only release

The abusive impulses
of a traumatized self

A need
for control

Strict
narratives

Definite
meanings

Imagined
perfection

The self-satisfying terror
of watching it all
crumble

Confirmation of my own
inadequacy

What makes me feel worse
makes me feel better

A struggle with abstraction
Tightness in my shoulders

For years I was drunk
or hungover

Drunk and
hungover

So tired

Tired and neglectful

About to throw up
or pass out

Explode
in barely

tamped-down anger

Overdoses

Accidents

Half my friends

from high school are dead

My survivor's guilt

is strong

I think of them often

Dream about them

The pain they must have been in

Their lives were difficult

much more than mine

I've been stalking them

on Facebook, their families

Which is probably natural

a way to grieve

inhabit the distance

and loss, make it feel real

fill in the years that went

by silent

One friend in particular,

the one I was closest to,

his heart went to one person

his kidney to another

his liver and lungs too damaged to go to anyone

There were calling hours

I didn't find out about

until it was too late

I'm told there were several pictures of me and him

that it was a nice service and I was missed

I want those pictures

Want to see that I was a presence

in his life

worth remembering

That we aren't

completely lost

to each other

Vanity and self-centeredness

Behind all this
vanity and self-centeredness is a need
for love

A simple human
need for love

I struggle
to express

Have spent my life failing
to satisfy

Failed to make myself

vulnerable enough
to satisfy

Everyone
is someone
to be afraid of

Every noise
a potential
disaster

What the brain does
is the proximate

cause of what
a person does

A final common pathway
of influences on behavior

I have a thought
I think of a terrifying

thing that happened
long ago

Emotional parts
of my brain activate

I secrete
stress hormones

A behavior
occurs

I become sensitive
to certain sensory cues

that trigger specific
neurons that go

back to the fetal
environment

to childhood experiences
when the brain was assembled

My father frantic
in the flames

consuming his flesh
His screams

My mother leaving me
with a neighbor

following my father
into the ambulance

Both of them
gone

*I've become who I am*

A storyline
taking shape

Text becoming body

Pain

        and love

                and disappointment—

how much I can take
and give

Not
give up

But my wife

I'm afraid
she's unhappy

That it's because of me
my emotional distance

How I'd like nothing more
than to be
closer

How uncomfortable
closeness makes me

We struggle

We love each other

It can be difficult to remember why we're together

We have children which, no matter what happens, binds us forever

We also have joint bank accounts, a mortgage and combined retirement plans

We have generally positive feelings about each other's parents and siblings, extended family and friends

> There's also love
> I love her more than any woman I've ever met
> or will
>
> That
> will never change

Our marriage—

a narrative

we step into and out of

inhabit and discuss

carefully construct and

take apart

misrepresent, correct

and misrepresent again—

it leaves such little

time for us

But that first night we spent together—

we talked a lot

And the next morning
we chain smoked cigarettes,
drank really strong coffee

I couldn't stop

You said
I had to go

That you needed time
to process what was happening

How do I describe what I felt then

A loss
of control

Fate
unfolding

A lack of choice
I fully embraced

*Who were we*
    *when we were*
        *who we were*
            *back then*

Before marriage and children, a mortgage

Before we knew how to love each other

The ways we can't

love each other adequately

but love nonetheless

That's what I want to know

Because those people we were need to know

that disillusionment is coming

They need to know and decide

to love each other regardless

to understand that the disillusionment

is where love becomes

strength

devotion to

the versions of ourselves we've known

have yet to know

Those people

from back then

have become us

And we

our present selves

now

in this new moment

moving forward

we

are together

Let's be

together now

The future terrifies

Care is a mammal emotion

Last night I dreamt I was Captain America

shitting himself

Today the "Imperial Theme" from Star Wars blares

from my neighborhood firehouse

"You look really sad,"

a stranger handing out flyers to a comedy show says to me

According to the book I'm reading,

"The universe is a finite thing

growing into something infinite

if you're willing to wait

an eternity"

We all mean well

I guess

Every child terrifies. When we first brought them home, I would hold either of my twin babies and wonder: if they died, where would they go? To think I would go nowhere when I died was fine. To think they would too was impossible. They were so little, just days old, their existence so strange and wonderful and new. Too perfect to endure.

I'd recently seen a movie, *The Curious Case of Benjamin Button*, in which the title character ages backward. The filmmakers went all the way with it, took Benjamin back to when he was a baby and, in one of the final scenes, while his ex-lover and now caretaker is holding him, the infant Button closes his eyes, peacefully, as if he were just going to sleep, but really he dies.

Or perhaps my preoccupation with death was a way to try and read, to comprehend, those first days of parenthood. The kind of reading Mary Ruefle says is an extension of time, and in which you "die and watch those you love die, until the very dizziness of it all becomes a source of compassion for ourselves, and for the language we created." Language. My children. My death obsession. A desire, Ruefle might say, to "make everything ok."

My son was two months old when he woke in the middle of the night crying in a way I'd never heard before, one that signaled something was very wrong.

I felt the heat coming off his head before I laid my hand on it.

At the hospital I was instructed to hold him still while he screamed and nurses stuck needles in him in numerous attempts to find a vein for his I.V.

They gave him a catheter. A spinal tap.

So stressful it gave me shingles.

Changed me.

For the first time I was fully there, present for someone in a way I'd never been. Present for him. The love I had for him was beyond anything I've ever felt. And I was fully aware of it.

I laid with him on a gurney after the nurses were done sticking needles in him. He threw up. I cleaned him up and he fell asleep. I stroked his cheek and promised over and over—said it out loud—that I would always, always, take care of him and his sister, that I'd always be there for them and never let anything bad happen.

Which is fucking ridiculous. Something I'll totally fail at. Totally am failing at. But it didn't matter. It's an impossible task. Love that intense. It's reliance on human fallibility.

I'm learning *the faith*
that it might all
be ok
that hopelessness and death
are ok
States of existence
over which
we have little control
It's all part of *the treatment*
The etymology of *story*
The words
that often escape me
Meta experience
that competes with
the experience
Minor versions
of disastrous behavior
Everybody wants to be better
but nobody has a baseline
for understanding themselves
God     Angels
I'm no longer
opposed to those words
I'm not sure
what that means

The brakes burning up
when we try
to slow down
Post-apocalyptic chic
after the real apocalypse
Look at me
like I'm important
I'm neither important
nor should you look at me
My ill
fitting clothes
All the words it takes
to figure out
what doesn't
need to be said

Things happen     The story evolves

We're in a church basement. I'm sober. The kids are participating in their first drama club, singing and dancing and acting and playing imaginary instruments. In a moment they will all—meaning all the kids in the drama class—sing "Sit Down You're Rocking the Boat." They—meaning my kids—have completed their first full week of kindergarten. They seem happy. They like school, they say. "We love it!" they say.

Which makes me feel good. I don't remember liking school. I remember an older kid I worshipped named Todd said he didn't like school and so I decided not to like it either. I remember being scared and nervous and uncomfortable and certain I was stupid.

When they're done singing the song and the show is over, my son wants me to carry him. My daughter wants me to carry her. I resist because they're heavy and it's hot and I'm lazy but then remember they're 5.5 years old. Soon neither will want to be carried and I will miss when they did, which is this moment. In the future I will miss this moment. So I carry them, one at a time, alternating each from one block to the next, until I'm tired, put them down and say, "you're big kids now. You can walk on your own." Which is true. But I wasn't *that* tired. I could have carried them further.

**Acknowledgments**

Grateful acknowledgment to the publications in which versions of poems from this book first appeared: *Academy of American Poets Poem-a-Day, Gramma, NOÖ Weekly, Philadelphia Review of Books, Powder Keg, Public Pool* and *Reality Beach*.

Thanks to Sommer Browning, Paula Cisewski, Jon-Michael Frank, Elisa Gabbert, Niina Pollari, Sampson Starkweather and Chris Tonelli for critical, careful, compassionate and honest readings of various versions of this book.

Eternal love and gratitude to Meri, Louisa and Henry—my hearts, my world.

Gratitude to Jeff F, Melissa B and Emily F for helping me to keep coming back.

Tom Lisk, poet, mentor and teacher, whose love and spirit I will carry with me always.

Thanks to my publisher and editor, Adam Robinson, for his time, care, attention and generosity in the process of making this book a reality.

To Chris, Joey, Tom and Tommy—old friends gone too soon.

Justin Marks' books are, *You're Going to Miss Me When You're Bored* (Barrelhouse Books, 2014) and *A Million in Prizes* (New Issues, 2009). He is a co-founder of Birds, LLC, an independent poetry press, and lives in New York City with his family.

www.ingramcontent.com/pod-product-compliance
Lightning Source LLC
Chambersburg PA
CBHW030349100526
44592CB00010B/880